To: Nicky

From: Angela
& Graham
xx

Date: Christmas 2018

Message:
God bless you dear friend
x

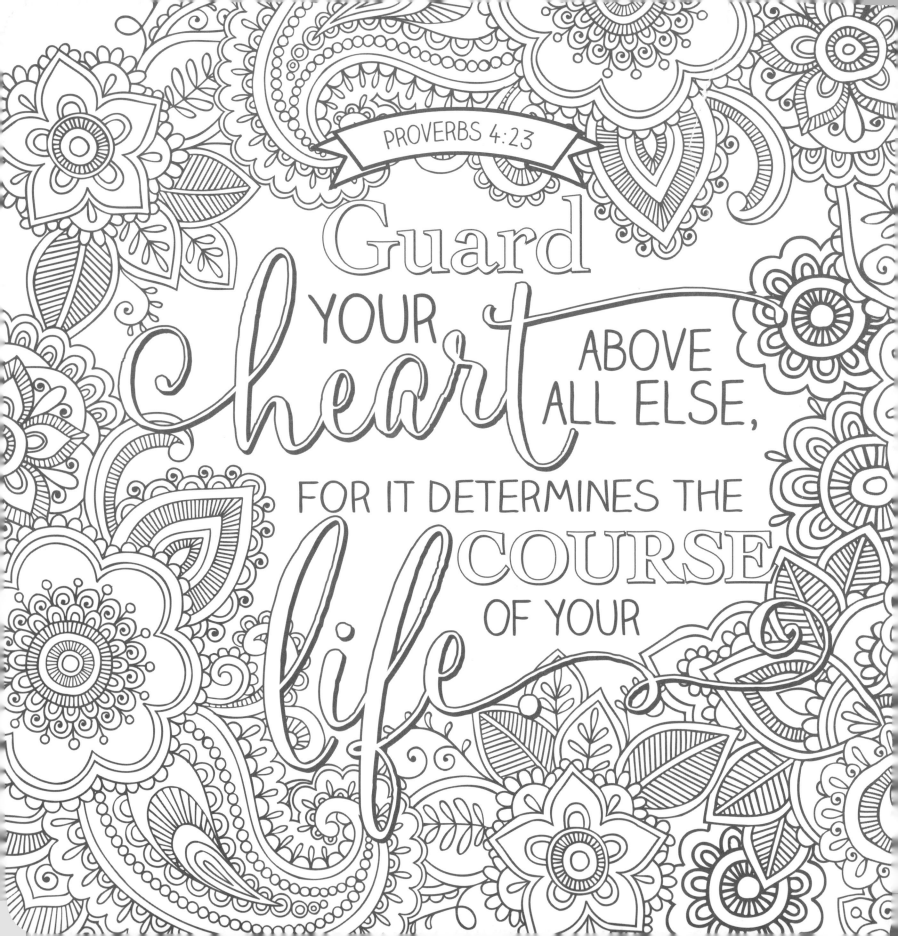

Inspire

Proverbs

NLT®

Tyndale House Publishers, Inc.
Carol Stream, Illinois

Published by Christian Art Publishers, PO Box 1599, Vereeniging, 1930, RSA.

Distributed by Tyndale House Publishers, Inc.

Extrabiblical artwork, cover design, and product design copyright © 2017 by Christian Art Publishers.

Images used under license from Shutterstock.com. All rights reserved.

This edition of *Inspire: Proverbs* is taken from the *Holy Bible*, New Living Translation, copyright © 1996, 2004, 2015 by Tyndale House Foundation. All rights reserved.

Visit Tyndale online at www.inspirebible.com, www.newlivingtranslation.com, and www.tyndale.com.

A full introduction to the NLT can be found at www.TheNLT.com/NLTIntro.

A complete list of the translators can be found at www.TheNLT.com/scholars.

ISBN 978-1-4964-2664-2 Softcover

Printed in China

26 25 24 23 22 21 20 19 18 17
10 9 8 7 6 5 4 3 2 1

Walk WITH THE wise AND become wise

PROVERBS 13:20

Welcome to Inspire: Proverbs!

The book of Proverbs is much loved because of its abundance of practical wisdom for life. Be inspired to honor God with right living as you color and creative journal through all 31 chapters of Proverbs and mine the riches and depth of its wisdom and instruction. ***Inspire: Proverbs*** offers creative space right alongside the biblical text for you to interact with Scripture in a unique, life-giving, hope-filled, and healing way— wherever you are on your faith journey! Scripture is God's inspired Word, and it leads us to a better understanding of him. It also teaches us about our identity and reveals God's intended purpose for our lives. It is fresh and relevant and powerful! Time spent in God's Word is time spent with God—and Bible journaling is breathing new life into Scripture reading.

Lingering in God's Word through coloring and art journaling not only plants his inspired works more deeply in our hearts and draws us closer to God; it also makes it easier to remember Scripture because we've made it personal through our art on the page. The process of coloring and art journaling engages our imaginations and invites us to reflect on Scripture as we envision how to express the key truths a passage teaches us about God. Our worshipful coloring and creative journaling reflects our faith journey and becomes a personal expression of God's movement in our lives. It is an expressive, artistic way of studying God's Word where the art becomes a reminder of how we are growing in our faith journey. When we journal in this way, we are creating a visual representation of what God is writing on our hearts through his Word. It becomes a way to remember and share with others what God is teaching us.

If you are new to Bible journaling, you may find this process helpful:

Pray

Ask the Holy Spirit to be present in your time in God's Word.

Read

Read a portion of Scripture.

Ask

What stands out in this passage?
What does this passage say about God?
How does this passage inform how I live?

Respond

Ask these three questions, and use your answers to create an image in the margins as a response to Scripture.
What images come to mind?
What phrase or verse will you highlight?
What colors come to mind?

There is no wrong way to be creative with your application of God's Word. So grab your favorite tools and get started!

May God bless you richly as you linger in the Proverbs and create a beautiful collection of your praise and worship on the pages of this book. It is sure to become a spiritual heirloom you will treasure for many years to come!

A *peaceful* HEART LEADS TO A *healthy* BODY.

PROVERBS 14:30

Proverbs

The Purpose of Proverbs

1 These are the proverbs of Solomon, David's son, king of Israel.

2 Their purpose is to teach people wisdom and discipline,
   to help them understand the insights of the wise.
3 Their purpose is to teach people to live disciplined and successful lives,
   to help them do what is right, just, and fair.
4 *These proverbs* will give
   insight to the simple, *knowledge*
   and discernment to the young.

5 Let the wise listen to these proverbs and become even wiser.
   Let those with understanding receive guidance
6 by exploring the meaning in these proverbs and parables,
   the words of the wise and their riddles.

7 Fear of the LORD is the foundation of true knowledge,
   but fools despise wisdom and discipline.

A Father's Exhortation: Acquire Wisdom
8 My child, listen when your father corrects you.
   Don't neglect your mother's instruction.
9 What you *learn* from them will crown
   you with *grace* and be a chain of *honor*
   around your neck.
10 My child, if sinners entice you,
   turn your back on them!
11 They may say, "Come and join us.
   Let's hide and kill someone!
   Just for fun, let's ambush the innocent!
12 Let's swallow them alive, like the grave;
   let's swallow them whole, like those who go down to the pit of death.
13 Think of the *great things* we'll get!
   We'll fill *our houses* with all the stuff we take.
14 Come, throw in your lot with us;
   we'll all share the loot."

¹⁵ My child, don't go along with them!
Stay far away from their paths.
¹⁶ They rush to commit evil deeds.
They hurry to commit murder.
¹⁷ If a bird sees a trap being set,
it knows to stay away.
¹⁸ But these people set an ambush for themselves;
they are trying to get themselves killed.
¹⁹ Such is the fate of all who are greedy for money;
it robs them of life.

Wisdom Shouts in the Streets

²⁰ Wisdom shouts in the streets.
She cries out in the public square.
²¹ She calls to the crowds along the main street,
to those gathered in front of the city gate:
²² "How long, you simpletons,
will you insist on being simpleminded?
How long will you mockers relish your mocking?
How long will you fools hate knowledge?

²³ *Come and listen* to my counsel.
I'll share my *heart with you*
and make you *wise.*

²⁴ "I called you so often, but you wouldn't come.
I reached out to you, but you paid no attention.
²⁵ You ignored my advice
and rejected the correction I offered.
²⁶ So I will laugh when you are in trouble!
I will mock you when disaster overtakes you—
²⁷ when calamity overtakes you like a storm,
when disaster engulfs you like a cyclone,
and anguish and distress overwhelm you.

²⁸ "When they cry for help, I will not answer.
Though they anxiously search for me, they will not
find me.
²⁹ For they hated knowledge
and chose not to fear the LORD.
³⁰ They rejected my advice
and paid no attention when I corrected them.
³¹ Therefore, they must eat the bitter fruit of living their own way,
choking on their own schemes.
³² For simpletons turn away from me—to death.
Fools are destroyed by their own complacency.

³³ But all who *listen* to me will
live in peace,
untroubled by fear of harm."

The Benefits of Wisdom

2 ¹ My child, listen to what I say,
  and treasure my commands.
² Tune your ears to wisdom,
  and concentrate on understanding.
³ Cry out for insight,
  and ask for understanding.
⁴ Search for them as you would for silver;
  seek them like hidden treasures.
⁵ Then you will understand what it means to fear the LORD,
  and you will gain knowledge of God.

⁶ *For the LORD grants wisdom!*
  From his mouth come
knowledge and understanding.

⁷ He grants a treasure of common sense to the honest.
  He is a shield to those who walk with integrity.
⁸ He guards the paths of the just
  and protects those who are faithful to him.

⁹ Then you will understand what is right, just, and fair,
  and you will find the right way to go.

¹⁰ *For wisdom will enter your heart,*
  and knowledge will fill you with joy.

¹¹ Wise choices will watch over you.
  Understanding will keep you safe.

¹² Wisdom will save you from evil people,
  from those whose words are twisted.
¹³ These men turn from the right way
  to walk down dark paths.
¹⁴ They take pleasure in doing wrong,
  and they enjoy the twisted ways of evil.
¹⁵ Their actions are crooked,
  and their ways are wrong.

¹⁶ Wisdom will save you from the immoral woman,
  from the seductive words of the promiscuous woman.
¹⁷ She has abandoned her husband
  and ignores the covenant she made before God.
¹⁸ Entering her house leads to death;
  it is the road to the grave.
¹⁹ The man who visits her is doomed.
  He will never reach the paths of life.

²⁰ *So follow the steps of the good,*

  and stay on the paths of the righteous.

So follow the steps of the GOOD, & stay on the paths of the RIGHTEOUS.

Proverbs 2:20

21 For only the *godly will live* in the land,
and those with *integrity* will remain in it.

22 But the wicked will be removed from the land,
and the treacherous will be uprooted.

Trusting in the LORD

3 **1** My child, never forget the things I have taught you.
Store my commands in your heart.
2 If you do this, you will live many years,
and your life will be satisfying.

3 Never let *loyalty and kindness* leave you!

Tie them around your neck as a *reminder*.

Write them deep within your *heart*.

4 Then you will find favor with both God and people,
and you will earn a good reputation.

5 *Trust in the LORD with all your heart;*

do not depend on your own *understanding*.

6 Seek his will in all you do,
and he will show you which path to take.

7 Don't be impressed with your own wisdom.
Instead, fear the LORD and turn away from evil.
8 Then you will have healing for your body
and strength for your bones.

9 Honor the LORD with your wealth
and with the best part of everything you produce.
10 Then he will fill your barns with grain,
and your vats will overflow with good wine.

11 My child, don't reject the LORD's discipline,
and don't be upset when he corrects you.
12 For the LORD corrects those he loves,
just as a father corrects a child in whom he delights.

13 Joyful is the person who finds wisdom,
the one who gains understanding.
14 For wisdom is more profitable than silver,
and her wages are better than gold.
15 Wisdom is more precious than rubies;
nothing you desire can compare with her.
16 She offers you long life in her right hand,
and riches and honor in her left.
17 She will guide you down delightful paths;
all her ways are satisfying.

¹⁸ Wisdom is a tree of life to those who embrace her;
      happy are those who hold her tightly.

¹⁹ By wisdom the LORD founded the earth;
      by understanding he created the heavens.
²⁰ By his knowledge the deep fountains of the earth burst forth,
      and the dew settles beneath the night sky.

²¹ My child, don't lose sight of common sense and discernment.
      Hang on to them,
²² for they will refresh your soul.
      They are like jewels on a necklace.
²³ They keep you safe on your way,
      and your feet will not stumble.
²⁴ You can go to bed without fear;
      you will lie down and sleep soundly.
²⁵ You need not be afraid of sudden disaster
      or the destruction that comes upon the wicked,
²⁶ for the LORD is your security.
      He will keep your foot from being caught in a trap.

²⁷ *Do not withhold good from those who deserve it when it's in your power to help them.*

²⁸ If you can help your neighbor now, don't say,
      "Come back tomorrow, and then I'll help you."

²⁹ Don't plot harm against your neighbor,
      for those who live nearby trust you.
³⁰ Don't pick a fight without reason,
      when no one has done you harm.

³¹ Don't envy violent people
      or copy their ways.
³² Such wicked people are detestable to the LORD,
      but he offers his friendship to the godly.

³³ The LORD curses the house of the wicked,
      but he blesses the home of the upright.

³⁴ The LORD mocks the mockers
      but is gracious to the humble.

³⁵ The wise inherit honor,
      but fools are put to shame!

A Father's Wise Advice

4 ¹ My children, listen when your father corrects you.
      Pay attention and learn good judgment,
² for I am giving you good guidance.
      Don't turn away from my instructions.
³ For I, too, was once my father's son,
      tenderly loved as my mother's only child.

⁴ My father taught me,
"Take my *words to heart.*
        Follow my commands, and you will **live.**
⁵ Get wisdom; develop good judgment.
    Don't forget my words or turn away from them.
⁶ Don't turn your back on wisdom, for she will protect you.
    Love her, and she will guard you.
⁷ Getting wisdom is the wisest thing you can do!
    And whatever else you do, develop good judgment.
⁸ If you prize wisdom, she will make you great.
    Embrace her, and she will honor you.
⁹ She will place a lovely wreath on your head;
    she will present you with a beautiful crown."

¹⁰ My child, listen to me and do as I say,
    and you will have a long, good life.
¹¹ I will teach you wisdom's ways
    and lead you in straight paths.
¹² When you walk, you won't be held back;
    when you run, you won't stumble.
¹³ Take hold of my instructions; don't let them go.
    Guard them, for they are the key to life.

¹⁴ Don't do as the wicked do,
    and don't follow the path of evildoers.
¹⁵ Don't even think about it; don't go that way.
    Turn away and keep moving.
¹⁶ For evil people can't sleep until they've done their evil deed for the day.
    They can't rest until they've caused someone to stumble.
¹⁷ They eat the food of wickedness
    and drink the wine of violence!

¹⁸ *The way of the* **righteous** *is like the*
    first gleam of dawn,
    which shines ever **brighter** until the full light of day.

¹⁹ But the way of the wicked is like total darkness.
    They have no idea what they are stumbling over.

²⁰ My child, pay attention to what I say.
    Listen carefully to my words.
²¹ Don't lose sight of them.
    Let them penetrate deep into your heart,
²² for they bring life to those who find them,
    and healing to their whole body.

²³ *Guard your heart above all else,*
        for it *determines* the course of *your life.*

²⁴ Avoid all perverse talk;
    stay away from corrupt speech.

The way of the RIGHTEOUS is like the first gleam of dawn, which shines ever brighter until the full light of day.

Proverbs 4:18

²⁵ Look straight ahead,
and fix your eyes on what lies before you.
²⁶ Mark out a straight path for your feet;
stay on the safe path.
²⁷ Don't get sidetracked;
keep your feet from following evil.

Avoid Immoral Women

5 ¹ My son, pay attention to my wisdom;
listen carefully to my wise counsel.
² Then you will show discernment,
and your lips will express what you've learned.
³ For the lips of an immoral woman are as sweet as honey,
and her mouth is smoother than oil.
⁴ But in the end she is as bitter as poison,
as dangerous as a double-edged sword.
⁵ Her feet go down to death;
her steps lead straight to the grave.
⁶ For she cares nothing about the path to life.
She staggers down a crooked trail and doesn't
realize it.

⁷ So now, my sons, listen to me.
Never stray from what I am about to say:
⁸ Stay away from her!
Don't go near the door of her house!
⁹ If you do, you will lose your honor
and will lose to merciless people all you have
achieved.
¹⁰ Strangers will consume your wealth,
and someone else will enjoy the fruit of your labor.
¹¹ In the end you will groan in anguish
when disease consumes your body.
¹² You will say, "How I hated discipline!
If only I had not ignored all the warnings!
¹³ Oh, why didn't I listen to my teachers?
Why didn't I pay attention to my instructors?
¹⁴ I have come to the brink of utter ruin,
and now I must face public disgrace."

¹⁵ Drink water from your own well—
share your love only with your wife.
¹⁶ Why spill the water of your springs in the streets,
having sex with just anyone?
¹⁷ You should reserve it for yourselves.
Never share it with strangers.
¹⁸ *Let your wife be a fountain of blessing for you.*
Rejoice in the wife of your youth.

¹⁹ She is a loving deer, a graceful doe.
  Let her breasts satisfy you always.
  May you always be captivated by her love.
²⁰ Why be captivated, my son, by an immoral woman,
  or fondle the breasts of a promiscuous woman?

²¹ For the LORD sees clearly what a man does,
  examining every path he takes.
²² An evil man is held captive by his own sins;
  they are ropes that catch and hold him.
²³ He will die for lack of self-control;
  he will be lost because of his great foolishness.

Lessons for Daily Life

6 ¹ My child, if you have put up security for a friend's debt
    or agreed to guarantee the debt of a stranger—
² if you have trapped yourself by your agreement
  and are caught by what you said—
³ follow my advice and save yourself,
  for you have placed yourself at your friend's mercy.
 Now swallow your pride;
  go and beg to have your name erased.
⁴ Don't put it off; do it now!
  Don't rest until you do.
⁵ Save yourself like a gazelle escaping from a
    hunter,
  like a bird fleeing from a net.

⁶ *Take a lesson from the ants, you lazybones.*

  *Learn from their ways
    and become wise!*
⁷ Though they have no prince
  or governor or ruler to make them work,
⁸ they labor hard all summer,
  gathering food for the winter.
⁹ But you, lazybones, how long will you sleep?
  When will you wake up?
¹⁰ A little extra sleep, a little more slumber,
  a little folding of the hands to rest—
¹¹ then poverty will pounce on you like a bandit;
  scarcity will attack you like an armed robber.

¹² What are worthless and wicked people like?
  They are constant liars,
¹³ signaling their deceit with a wink of the eye,
  a nudge of the foot, or the wiggle of fingers.
¹⁴ Their perverted hearts plot evil,
  and they constantly stir up trouble.
¹⁵ But they will be destroyed suddenly,
  broken in an instant beyond all hope of healing.

FOR THE LORD SEES clearly WHAT A MAN DOES, EXAMINING EVERY path HE TAKES.

PROVERBS 5:21

16 There are six things the LORD hates—
  no, seven things he detests:
17 haughty eyes,
  a lying tongue,
  hands that kill the innocent,
18 a heart that plots evil,
  feet that race to do wrong,
19 a false witness who pours out lies,
  a person who sows discord in a family.

20 *My son, obey your father's commands,*
  and don't neglect your mother's instruction.

21 Keep their words always in your heart.
  Tie them around your neck.
22 When you walk, their counsel will lead you.
  When you sleep, they will protect you.
  When you wake up, they will advise you.
23 For their command is a lamp
  and their instruction a light;
 their corrective discipline
  is the way to life.
24 It will keep you from the immoral woman,
  from the smooth tongue of a promiscuous woman.
25 Don't lust for her beauty.
  Don't let her coy glances seduce you.
26 For a prostitute will bring you to poverty,
  but sleeping with another man's wife will cost you
    your life.
27 Can a man scoop a flame into his lap
  and not have his clothes catch on fire?
28 Can he walk on hot coals
  and not blister his feet?
29 So it is with the man who sleeps with another man's wife.
  He who embraces her will not go unpunished.

30 Excuses might be found for a thief
  who steals because he is starving.
31 But if he is caught, he must pay back seven times what he stole,
  even if he has to sell everything in his house.
32 But the man who commits adultery is an utter fool,
  for he destroys himself.
33 He will be wounded and disgraced.
  His shame will never be erased.
34 For the woman's jealous husband will be furious,
  and he will show no mercy when he takes revenge.
35 He will accept no compensation,
  nor be satisfied with a payoff of any size.

Another Warning about Immoral Women

7 [1] Follow my advice, my son;
always treasure my commands.
[2] Obey my commands and live!
Guard my instructions as you guard your own eyes.
[3] Tie them on your fingers as a reminder.
Write them deep within your heart.

[4] *Love wisdom like a sister; make insight a beloved member of your family.*

[5] Let them protect you from an affair with an immoral woman,
from listening to the flattery of a promiscuous woman.

[6] While I was at the window of my house,
looking through the curtain,
[7] I saw some naive young men,
and one in particular who lacked common sense.
[8] He was crossing the street near the house of an immoral
woman,
strolling down the path by her house.
[9] It was at twilight, in the evening,
as deep darkness fell.
[10] The woman approached him,
seductively dressed and sly of heart.
[11] She was the brash, rebellious type,
never content to stay at home.
[12] She is often in the streets and markets,
soliciting at every corner.
[13] She threw her arms around him and kissed him,
and with a brazen look she said,
[14] "I've just made my peace offerings
and fulfilled my vows.

Follow my advice, my son; **ALWAYS TREASURE MY COMMANDS.** Obey my commands & *live!* Proverbs 7:1-2

¹⁵ You're the one I was looking for!
    I came out to find you, and here you are!
¹⁶ My bed is spread with beautiful blankets,
    with colored sheets of Egyptian linen.
¹⁷ I've perfumed my bed
    with myrrh, aloes, and cinnamon.
¹⁸ Come, let's drink our fill of love until morning.
    Let's enjoy each other's caresses,
¹⁹ for my husband is not home.
    He's away on a long trip.
²⁰ He has taken a wallet full of money with him
    and won't return until later this month."

²¹ So she seduced him with her pretty speech
    and enticed him with her flattery.
²² He followed her at once,
    like an ox going to the slaughter.
  He was like a stag caught in a trap,
²³   awaiting the arrow that would pierce its heart.
  He was like a bird flying into a snare,
    little knowing it would cost him his life.

²⁴ So listen to me, my sons,
    and pay attention to my words.
²⁵ Don't let your hearts stray away toward her.
    Don't wander down her wayward path.
²⁶ For she has been the ruin of many;
    many men have been her victims.
²⁷ Her house is the road to the grave.
    Her bedroom is the den of death.

Wisdom Calls for a Hearing

8 ¹ Listen as Wisdom calls out!
    Hear as understanding raises her voice!
² On the hilltop along the road,
    she takes her stand at the crossroads.
³ By the gates at the entrance to the town,
    on the road leading in, she cries aloud,
⁴ "I call to you, to all of you!
    I raise my voice to all people.
⁵ You simple people, use good judgment.
    You foolish people, show some understanding.
⁶ Listen to me! For I have important things to tell you.
    Everything I say is right,
⁷ for I speak the truth
    and detest every kind of deception.
⁸ My advice is wholesome.
    There is nothing devious or crooked in it.
⁹ *My words* are plain to *anyone* with
           understanding,
clear to those with *knowledge.*

[10] Choose my instruction rather than silver,
and knowledge rather than pure gold.

[11] *For wisdom* is far more valuable than *rubies.*

Nothing you *desire* can **compare** with it.

[12] "I, Wisdom, live together with good judgment.
I know where to discover knowledge and
discernment.
[13] All who fear the LORD will hate evil.
Therefore, I hate pride and arrogance,
corruption and perverse speech.
[14] Common sense and success belong to me.
Insight and strength are mine.
[15] Because of me, kings reign,
and rulers make just decrees.
[16] Rulers lead with my help,
and nobles make righteous judgments.

[17] "I love all who love me.
Those who search will surely find me.
[18] I have riches and honor,
as well as enduring wealth and justice.

[19] *My gifts* are better than *gold,* even the purest gold,

my wages **better than sterling silver!**

[20] I walk in righteousness,
in paths of justice.
[21] Those who love me inherit wealth.
I will fill their treasuries.

[22] "The LORD formed me from the beginning,
before he created anything else.
[23] I was appointed in ages past,
at the very first, before the earth began.
[24] I was born before the oceans were created,
before the springs bubbled forth their waters.
[25] Before the mountains were formed,
before the hills, I was born—
[26] before he had made the earth and fields
and the first handfuls of soil.
[27] I was there when he established the heavens,
when he drew the horizon on the oceans.
[28] I was there when he set the clouds above,
when he established springs deep in the earth.
[29] I was there when he set the limits of the seas,
so they would not spread beyond their boundaries.
And when he marked off the earth's foundations,
[30]   I was the architect at his side.
I was his constant delight,
rejoicing always in his presence.

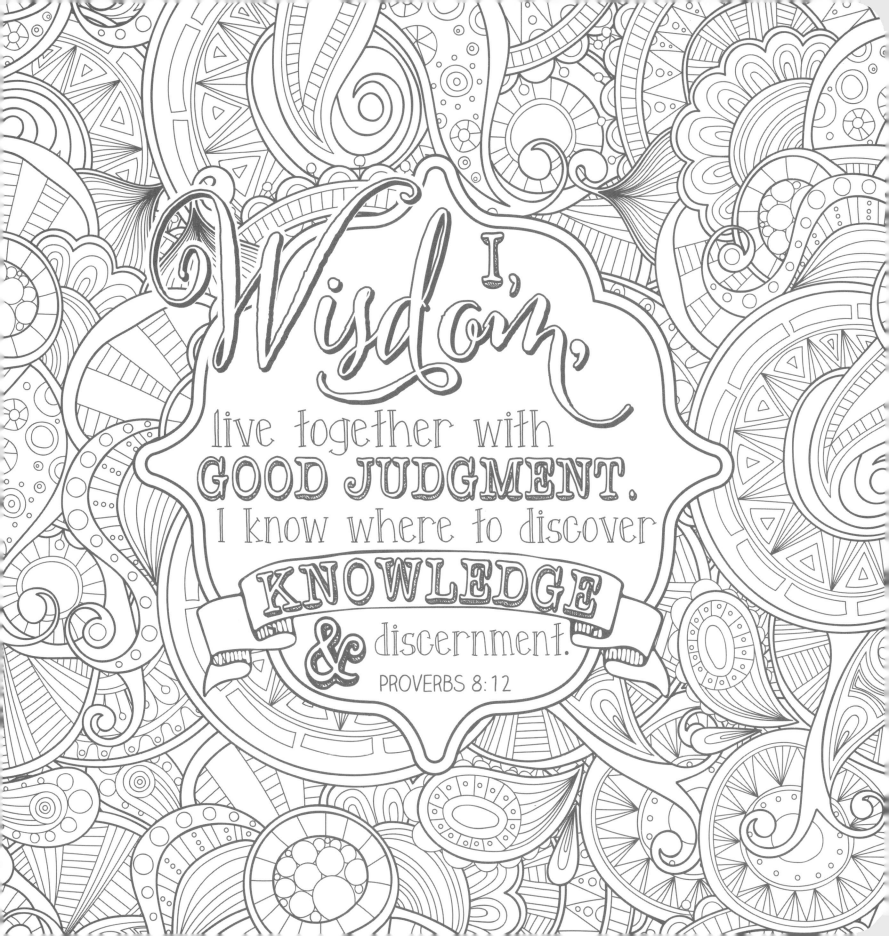

I, *Wisdom,* live together with **GOOD JUDGMENT.** I know where to discover **KNOWLEDGE** & discernment.

PROVERBS 8:12

31 And how happy I was with the world he created;
    how I rejoiced with the human family!

32 "And so, my children, listen to me,
    for all who follow my ways are joyful.
33 Listen to my instruction and be wise.
    Don't ignore it.
34 Joyful are those who listen to me,
    watching for me daily at my gates,
    waiting for me outside my home!
35 For whoever finds me finds life
    and receives favor from the LORD.
36 But those who miss me injure themselves.
    All who hate me love death."

9 **1** Wisdom has built her house;
    she has carved its seven columns.
 2 She has prepared a great banquet,
    mixed the wines, and set the table.
 3 She has sent her servants to invite everyone to come.
    She calls out from the heights overlooking the city.
 4 "Come in with me," she urges the simple.
    To those who lack good judgment, she says,
 5 "Come, eat my food,
    and drink the wine I have mixed.
 6 Leave your simple ways behind, and begin to live;
    learn to use good judgment."

 7 Anyone who rebukes a mocker will get an insult in return.
    Anyone who corrects the wicked will get hurt.
 8 So don't bother correcting mockers;
    they will only hate you.
  But correct the wise,
    and they will love you.
 9 Instruct the wise,
    and they will be even wiser.
  Teach the righteous,
    and they will learn even more.

10 Fear of the *LORD* is the *foundation of wisdom*.
    Knowledge of the *Holy One* results in good judgment.

11 Wisdom will multiply your days
    and add years to your life.
12 If you become wise, you will be the one to benefit.
    If you scorn wisdom, you will be the one to suffer.

Folly Calls for a Hearing

13 The woman named Folly is brash.
    She is ignorant and doesn't know it.
14 She sits in her doorway
    on the heights overlooking the city.

¹⁵ She calls out to men going by
who are minding their own business.
¹⁶ "Come in with me," she urges the simple.
To those who lack good judgment, she says,
¹⁷ "Stolen water is refreshing;
food eaten in secret tastes the best!"
¹⁸ But little do they know that the dead are there.
Her guests are in the depths of the grave.

The Proverbs of Solomon

10

The proverbs of Solomon:

A wise child brings joy to a father;
a foolish child brings grief to a mother.

² Tainted wealth has no lasting value,
but right living can save your life.

³ The LORD will not let the godly go hungry,
but he refuses to satisfy the craving of the wicked.

⁴ Lazy people are soon poor;
hard workers get rich.

⁵ A wise youth harvests in the summer,
but one who sleeps during harvest is a disgrace.

⁶ *The godly* are showered with *blessings;*

the *words* of the wicked

conceal violent intentions.

⁷ We have happy memories of the godly,
but the name of a wicked person rots away.

⁸ The wise are glad to be instructed,
but babbling fools fall flat on their faces.

⁹ People with integrity walk safely,
but those who follow crooked paths will be
exposed.

¹⁰ People who wink at wrong cause trouble,
but a bold reproof promotes peace.

¹¹ *The words* of the godly are a *life-giving fountain;*

the words of the wicked

conceal violent intentions.

¹² Hatred stirs up quarrels,
but love makes up for all offenses.

¹³ Wise words come from the lips of people with understanding,
but those lacking sense will be beaten with a rod.

THE godly ARE SHOWERED WITH blessings

PROVERBS 10:6

¹⁴ Wise people treasure knowledge,
but the babbling of a fool invites disaster.

¹⁵ The wealth of the rich is their fortress;
the poverty of the poor is their destruction.

¹⁶ The earnings of the godly enhance their lives,
but evil people squander their money on sin.

¹⁷ *People who* accept discipline are on the pathway to *life,*

but those *who ignore correction* will go astray.

¹⁸ Hiding hatred makes you a liar;
slandering others makes you a fool.

¹⁹ Too much talk leads to sin.
Be sensible and keep your mouth shut.

²⁰ The words of the godly are like sterling silver;
the heart of a fool is worthless.

²¹ The words of the godly encourage many,
but fools are destroyed by their lack of common sense.

²² *The blessing* of the *LORD*

makes a person rich, and he adds no sorrow with it.

²³ Doing wrong is fun for a fool,
but living wisely brings pleasure to the sensible.

²⁴ The fears of the wicked will be fulfilled;
the hopes of the godly will be granted.

²⁵ When the storms of life come, the wicked are whirled away,
but the godly have a lasting foundation.

The blessing of the LORD makes a person rich.

Proverbs 10:22

26 Lazy people irritate their employers,
   like vinegar to the teeth or smoke in the eyes.

27 Fear of the LORD lengthens one's life,
   but the years of the wicked are cut short.

28 The hopes of the godly result in happiness,
   but the expectations of the wicked come to nothing.

29 The way of the LORD is a stronghold to those with integrity,
   but it destroys the wicked.

30 The godly will never be disturbed,
   but the wicked will be removed from the land.

31 The mouth of the godly person gives wise advice,
   but the tongue that deceives will be cut off.

32 The lips of the godly speak helpful words,
   but the mouth of the wicked speaks perverse words.

11

1 The LORD detests the use of dishonest scales,
   but he delights in accurate weights.

2 Pride leads to disgrace,
   but with humility comes wisdom.

3 Honesty guides good people;
   dishonesty destroys treacherous people.

4 Riches won't help on the day of judgment,
   but right living can save you from death.

5 *The godly* are directed by *honesty;*

   *the wicked fall **beneath** their load of sin.*

6 The godliness of good people rescues them;
   the ambition of treacherous people traps them.

7 When the wicked die, their hopes die with them,
   for they rely on their own feeble strength.

8 The godly are rescued from trouble,
   and it falls on the wicked instead.

9 With their words, the godless destroy their friends,
   but knowledge will rescue the righteous.

10 The whole city celebrates when the godly succeed;
   they shout for joy when the wicked die.

11 Upright citizens are good for a city and make it prosper,
   but the talk of the wicked tears it apart.

12 It is foolish to belittle one's neighbor;
   a sensible person keeps quiet.

13 A gossip goes around telling secrets,
   but those who are trustworthy can keep a confidence.

14 Without wise leadership, a nation falls;
   there is safety in having many advisers.

¹⁵ There's danger in putting up security for a stranger's debt;
    it's safer not to guarantee another person's debt.

¹⁶ A gracious woman gains respect,
    but ruthless men gain only wealth.

¹⁷ Your kindness will reward you,
    but your cruelty will destroy you.

¹⁸ Evil people get rich for the moment,
    but the reward of the godly will last.

¹⁹ Godly people find life;
    evil people find death.

²⁰ The LORD detests people with crooked hearts,
    but he delights in those with integrity.

²¹ Evil people will surely be punished,
    but the children of the godly will go free.

²² A beautiful woman who lacks discretion
    is like a gold ring in a pig's snout.

²³ The godly can look forward to a reward,
    while the wicked can expect only judgment.

²⁴ Give freely and become more wealthy;
    be stingy and lose everything.

²⁵ The generous will prosper;
    those who refresh others will themselves be
      refreshed.

²⁶ People curse those who hoard their grain,
    but they bless the one who sells in time of need.

²⁷ If you search for good, you will find favor;
    but if you search for evil, it will find you!

²⁸ Trust in your money and down you go!
    But the godly flourish like leaves in spring.

²⁹ Those who bring trouble on their families inherit the wind.
    The fool will be a servant to the wise.

³⁰ The seeds of good deeds become a tree of life;
    a wise person wins friends.

³¹ If the righteous are rewarded here on earth,
    what will happen to wicked sinners?

12 ¹ To learn, you must love discipline;
    it is stupid to hate correction.

² The LORD approves of those who are good,
    but he condemns those who plan wickedness.

³ Wickedness never brings stability,
    but the godly have deep roots.

⁴ A worthy wife is a crown for her husband,
    but a disgraceful woman is like cancer in his bones.

The
generous
will prosper;
those who refresh others
will themselves
be
refreshed.

Proverbs 11:25

5 The plans of the godly are just;
the advice of the wicked is treacherous.

6 The words of the wicked are like a murderous ambush,
but the words of the godly save lives.

7 The wicked die and disappear,
but the family of the godly stands firm.

8 A sensible person wins admiration,
but a warped mind is despised.

9 Better to be an ordinary person with a servant
than to be self-important but have no food.

10 The godly care for their animals,
but the wicked are always cruel.

11 A hard worker has plenty of food,
but a person who chases fantasies has no sense.

12 Thieves are jealous of each other's loot,
but the godly are well rooted and bear their own fruit.

13 The wicked are trapped by their own words,
but the godly escape such trouble.

14 *Wise words* bring many *benefits,*
and *hard work* brings *rewards.*

15 Fools think their own way is right,
but the wise listen to others.

16 A fool is quick-tempered,
but a wise person stays calm when insulted.

17 An honest witness tells the truth;
a false witness tells lies.

18 Some people make cutting remarks,
but the words of the wise bring healing.

19 Truthful words stand the test of time,
but lies are soon exposed.

20 Deceit fills hearts that are plotting evil;
joy fills hearts that are planning peace!

21 No harm comes to the godly,
but the wicked have their fill of trouble.

22 The Lord detests lying lips,
but he delights in those who tell the truth.

23 The wise don't make a show of their knowledge,
but fools broadcast their foolishness.

24 Work hard and become a leader;
be lazy and become a slave.

25 Worry weighs a person down;
an encouraging word cheers a person up.

26 The godly give good advice to their friends;
   the wicked lead them astray.

27 Lazy people don't even cook the game they catch,
   but the diligent make use of everything they find.

28 The way of the *godly leads to life;*
   that path does not lead to death.

13 1 A wise child accepts a parent's discipline;
   a mocker refuses to listen to correction.

2 Wise words will win you a good meal,
   but treacherous people have an appetite for
   violence.

3 Those who control their tongue will have a long life;
   opening your mouth can ruin everything.

4 Lazy people want much but get little,
   but those who work hard will prosper.

5 The godly hate lies;
   the wicked cause shame and disgrace.

6 Godliness guards the path of the blameless,
   but the evil are misled by sin.

7 Some who are poor pretend to be rich;
   others who are rich pretend to be poor.

8 The rich can pay a ransom for their lives,
   but the poor won't even get threatened.

9 The life of the godly is full of light and joy,
   but the light of the wicked will be snuffed out.

10 Pride leads to conflict;
   those who take advice are wise.

11 Wealth from get-rich-quick schemes quickly disappears;
   wealth from hard work grows over time.

12 *Hope* deferred makes the *heart* sick,

   but a *dream fulfilled* is a tree of *life.*

13 People who despise advice are asking for trouble;
   those who respect a command will succeed.

14 The instruction of the wise is like a life-giving fountain;
   those who accept it avoid the snares of death.

15 A person with good sense is respected;
   a treacherous person is headed for destruction.

Hope DEFERRED MAKES THE HEART SICK, BUT A dream fulfilled is a TREE of life.

PROVERBS 13:12

THOSE WHO FOLLOW THE *right* PATH FEAR THE *Lord.*

PROVERBS 14:2

16 Wise people think before they act;
　　fools don't—and even brag about their foolishness.

17 An unreliable messenger stumbles into trouble,
　　but a reliable messenger brings healing.

18 If you ignore criticism, you will end in poverty and disgrace;
　　if you accept correction, you will be honored.

19 It is pleasant to see dreams come true,
　　but fools refuse to turn from evil to attain them.

20 Walk with the wise and become wise;
　　associate with fools and get in trouble.

21 Trouble chases sinners,
　　while blessings reward the righteous.

22 Good people leave an inheritance to their grandchildren,
　　but the sinner's wealth passes to the godly.

23 A poor person's farm may produce much food,
　　but injustice sweeps it all away.

24 Those who spare the rod of discipline hate their children.
　　Those who love their children care enough to discipline them.

25 The godly eat to their hearts' content,
　　but the belly of the wicked goes hungry.

14 1 A wise woman builds her home,
　　but a foolish woman tears it down with her own hands.

2 *Those who* follow the *right path* fear the *Lord;*

　　those who take the wrong path despise him.

3 A fool's proud talk becomes a rod that beats him,
　　but the words of the wise keep them safe.

4 Without oxen a stable stays clean,
　　but you need a strong ox for a large harvest.

5 An honest witness does not lie;
　　a false witness breathes lies.

6 A mocker seeks wisdom and never finds it,
　　but knowledge comes easily to those with understanding.

7 Stay away from fools,
　　for you won't find knowledge on their lips.

8 The prudent understand where they are going,
　　but fools deceive themselves.

9 Fools make fun of guilt,
　　but the godly acknowledge it and seek reconciliation.

10 Each heart knows its own bitterness,
　　and no one else can fully share its joy.

11 The house of the wicked will be destroyed,
   but the tent of the godly will flourish.

12 There is a path before each person that seems right,
   but it ends in death.

13 Laughter can conceal a heavy heart,
   but when the laughter ends, the grief remains.

14 Backsliders get what they deserve;
   good people receive their reward.

15 Only simpletons believe everything they're told!
   The prudent carefully consider their steps.

16 The wise are cautious and avoid danger;
   fools plunge ahead with reckless confidence.

17 Short-tempered people do foolish things,
   and schemers are hated.

18 Simpletons are clothed with foolishness,
   but the prudent are crowned with knowledge.

19 Evil people will bow before good people;
   the wicked will bow at the gates of the godly.

20 The poor are despised even by their neighbors,
   while the rich have many "friends."

21 It is a sin to belittle one's neighbor;
   blessed are those who help the poor.

22 *If you plan to do evil, you will be lost;*
   if you plan to do good, you will receive
   unfailing love & faithfulness.

23 Work brings profit,
   but mere talk leads to poverty!

24 Wealth is a crown for the wise;
   the effort of fools yields only foolishness.

25 A truthful witness saves lives,
   but a false witness is a traitor.

26 Those who fear the LORD are secure;
   he will be a refuge for their children.

27 Fear of the LORD is a life-giving fountain;
   it offers escape from the snares of death.

28 A growing population is a king's glory;
   a prince without subjects has nothing.

29 People with understanding control their anger;
   a hot temper shows great foolishness.

30 A peaceful heart leads to a healthy body;
   jealousy is like cancer in the bones.

³¹ Those who oppress the poor insult their Maker,
   but helping the poor honors him.

³² The wicked are crushed by disaster,
   but the godly have a refuge when they die.

³³ Wisdom is enshrined in an understanding heart;
   wisdom is not found among fools.

³⁴ Godliness makes a nation great,
   but sin is a disgrace to any people.

³⁵ A king rejoices in wise servants
   but is angry with those who disgrace him.

15 ¹ A gentle answer deflects anger,
   but harsh words make tempers flare.

² The tongue of the wise makes knowledge appealing,
   but the mouth of a fool belches out foolishness.

³ The LORD is watching everywhere,
   keeping his eye on both the evil and the good.

⁴ Gentle words are a tree of life;
   a deceitful tongue crushes the spirit.

⁵ Only a fool despises a parent's discipline;
   whoever learns from correction is wise.

⁶ There is treasure in the house of the godly,
   but the earnings of the wicked bring trouble.

⁷ The lips of the wise give good advice;
   the heart of a fool has none to give.

⁸ The LORD detests the sacrifice of the wicked,
   but he delights in the prayers of the upright.

⁹ The LORD detests the way of the wicked,
   but he loves those who pursue godliness.

¹⁰ Whoever abandons the right path will be severely
   disciplined;
   whoever hates correction will die.

¹¹ Even Death and Destruction hold no secrets from
   the LORD.
   How much more does he know the human heart!

¹² Mockers hate to be corrected,
   so they stay away from the wise.

¹³ A glad heart makes a happy face;
   a broken heart crushes the spirit.

¹⁴ A wise person is hungry for knowledge,
   while the fool feeds on trash.

¹⁵ For the despondent, every day brings trouble;
   for the happy heart, life is a continual feast.

¹⁶ Better to have little, with fear for the LORD,
   than to have great treasure and inner turmoil.

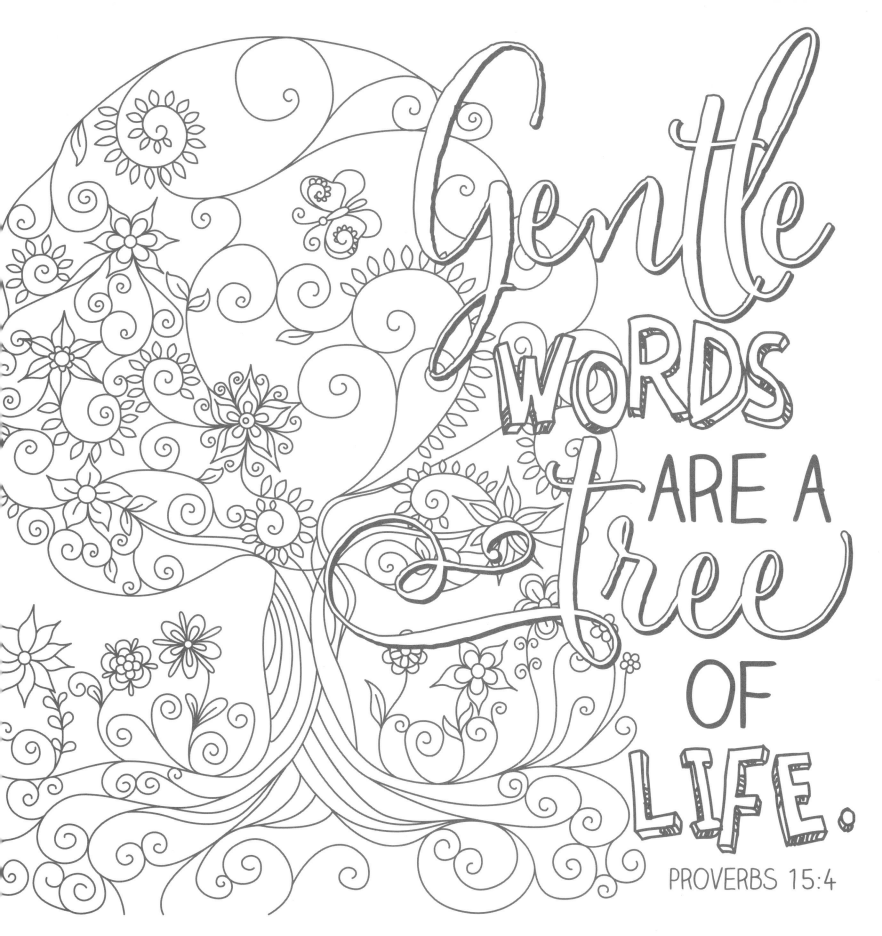

Gentle words are a tree of life.

PROVERBS 15:4

THE *heart* OF THE GODLY THINKS *carefully* BEFORE speaking

PROVERBS 15:28

¹⁷ A bowl of vegetables with someone you love
is better than steak with someone you hate.

¹⁸ A hot-tempered person starts fights;
a cool-tempered person stops them.

¹⁹ A lazy person's way is blocked with briers,
but the path of the upright is an open highway.

²⁰ Sensible children bring joy to their father;
foolish children despise their mother.

²¹ Foolishness brings joy to those with no sense;
a sensible person stays on the right path.

²² Plans go wrong for lack of advice;
many advisers bring success.

²³ *Everyone enjoys a fitting reply;
it is wonderful to say the right thing
at the right time!*

²⁴ The path of life leads upward for the wise;
they leave the grave behind.

²⁵ The LORD tears down the house of the proud,
but he protects the property of widows.

²⁶ The LORD detests evil plans,
but he delights in pure words.

²⁷ Greed brings grief to the whole family,
but those who hate bribes will live.

²⁸ The heart of the godly thinks carefully before speaking;
the mouth of the wicked overflows with evil words.

²⁹ The LORD is far from the wicked,
but he hears the prayers of the righteous.

³⁰ A cheerful look brings joy to the heart;
good news makes for good health.

³¹ *If you listen to constructive criticism,
you will be at home among the wise.*

³² If you reject discipline, you only harm yourself;
but if you listen to correction, you grow in understanding.

³³ *Fear of the LORD teaches wisdom;
humility precedes honor.*

16 ¹ We can make our own plans,
　　but the LORD gives the right answer.

² People may be pure in their own eyes,
　　but the LORD examines their motives.

³ *Commit your actions to the LORD,*

　　and your plans will succeed.

⁴ The LORD has made everything for his own purposes,
　　even the wicked for a day of disaster.

⁵ The LORD detests the proud;
　　they will surely be punished.

⁶ Unfailing love and faithfulness make atonement for sin.
　　By fearing the LORD, people avoid evil.

⁷ When people's lives please the LORD,
　　even their enemies are at peace with them.

⁸ Better to have little, with godliness,
　　than to be rich and dishonest.

⁹ We can make our plans,
　　but the LORD determines our steps.

¹⁰ The king speaks with divine wisdom;
　　he must never judge unfairly.

¹¹ The LORD demands accurate scales and balances;
　　he sets the standards for fairness.

¹² A king detests wrongdoing,
　　for his rule is built on justice.

¹³ The king is pleased with words from righteous lips;
　　he loves those who speak honestly.

¹⁴ The anger of the king is a deadly threat;
　　the wise will try to appease it.

¹⁵ When the king smiles, there is life;
　　his favor refreshes like a spring rain.

¹⁶ How much better to get wisdom than gold,
　　and good judgment than silver!

¹⁷ The path of the virtuous leads away from evil;
　　whoever follows that path is safe.

¹⁸ Pride goes before destruction,
　　and haughtiness before a fall.

¹⁹ Better to live humbly with the poor
　　than to share plunder with the proud.

²⁰ Those who listen to instruction will prosper;
　　those who trust the LORD will be joyful.

Kind words are like honey —
sweet to the soul and healthy for the body.

Proverbs 16:24

21 The wise are known for their understanding,
and pleasant words are persuasive.

22 Discretion is a life-giving fountain to those who possess it,
but discipline is wasted on fools.

23 From a wise mind comes wise speech;
the words of the wise are persuasive.

24 Kind words are like honey —

sweet to the soul & healthy for the body.

25 There is a path before each person that seems right,
but it ends in death.

26 It is good for workers to have an appetite;
an empty stomach drives them on.

27 Scoundrels create trouble;
their words are a destructive blaze.

28 A troublemaker plants seeds of strife;
gossip separates the best of friends.

29 Violent people mislead their companions,
leading them down a harmful path.

30 With narrowed eyes, people plot evil;
with a smirk, they plan their mischief.

31 Gray hair is a crown of glory;

it is gained by living a godly life.

32 Better to be patient than powerful;
better to have self-control than to conquer a city.

33 We may throw the dice,
but the LORD determines how they fall.

17 ¹ Better a dry crust eaten in peace
than a house filled with feasting—and conflict.

² A wise servant will rule over the master's disgraceful son
and will share the inheritance of the master's
children.

³ Fire tests the purity of silver and gold,
but the LORD tests the heart.

⁴ Wrongdoers eagerly listen to gossip;
liars pay close attention to slander.

⁵ Those who mock the poor insult their Maker;
those who rejoice at the misfortune of others will
be punished.

⁶ Grandchildren are the crowning glory of the aged;
    parents are the pride of their children.

⁷ Eloquent words are not fitting for a fool;
    even less are lies fitting for a ruler.

⁸ A bribe is like a lucky charm;
    whoever gives one will prosper!

⁹ Love prospers when a fault is forgiven,
    but dwelling on it separates close friends.

¹⁰ A single rebuke does more for a person of understanding
    than a hundred lashes on the back of a fool.

¹¹ Evil people are eager for rebellion,
    but they will be severely punished.

¹² It is safer to meet a bear robbed of her cubs
    than to confront a fool caught in foolishness.

¹³ If you repay good with evil,
    evil will never leave your house.

¹⁴ Starting a quarrel is like opening a floodgate,
    so stop before a dispute breaks out.

¹⁵ Acquitting the guilty and condemning the innocent—
    both are detestable to the LORD.

¹⁶ It is senseless to pay to educate a fool,
    since he has no heart for learning.

¹⁷ *A friend is always loyal,*
    and a brother is born to help in time of need.

¹⁸ It's poor judgment to guarantee another person's debt
    or put up security for a friend.

¹⁹ Anyone who loves to quarrel loves sin;
    anyone who trusts in high walls invites disaster.

²⁰ The crooked heart will not prosper;
    the lying tongue tumbles into trouble.

²¹ It is painful to be the parent of a fool;
    there is no joy for the father of a rebel.

²² A cheerful heart is good medicine,
    but a broken spirit saps a person's strength.

²³ The wicked take secret bribes
    to pervert the course of justice.

²⁴ Sensible people keep their eyes glued on wisdom,
    but a fool's eyes wander to the ends of the earth.

²⁵ Foolish children bring grief to their father
    and bitterness to the one who gave them birth.

²⁶ It is wrong to punish the godly for being good
    or to flog leaders for being honest.

²⁷ A truly wise person uses few words;
    a person with understanding is even-tempered.

²⁸ Even fools are thought wise when they keep silent;
    with their mouths shut, they seem intelligent.

18 ¹ Unfriendly people care only about themselves;
    they lash out at common sense.

² Fools have no interest in understanding;
    they only want to air their own opinions.

³ Doing wrong leads to disgrace,
    and scandalous behavior brings contempt.

⁴ *Wise words* are like deep waters;
    wisdom flows from the wise like a *bubbling brook.*

⁵ It is not right to acquit the guilty
    or deny justice to the innocent.

⁶ Fools' words get them into constant quarrels;
    they are asking for a beating.

⁷ The mouths of fools are their ruin;
    they trap themselves with their lips.

⁸ Rumors are dainty morsels
    that sink deep into one's heart.

⁹ A lazy person is as bad as
    someone who destroys things.

¹⁰ The name of the LORD is a strong fortress;
    the godly run to him and are safe.

¹¹ The rich think of their wealth as a strong defense;
    they imagine it to be a high wall of safety.

¹² Haughtiness goes before destruction;
    humility precedes honor.

¹³ Spouting off before listening to the facts
    is both shameful and foolish.

¹⁴ The human spirit can endure a sick body,
    but who can bear a crushed spirit?

¹⁵ Intelligent people are always ready to learn.
    Their ears are open for knowledge.

¹⁶ Giving a gift can open doors;
    it gives access to important people!

¹⁷ The first to speak in court sounds right—
    until the cross-examination begins.

¹⁸ Flipping a coin can end arguments;
    it settles disputes between powerful opponents.

¹⁹ An offended friend is harder to win back than a fortified city.
   Arguments separate friends like a gate locked with bars.

²⁰ Wise words satisfy like a good meal;
   the right words bring satisfaction.

²¹ The tongue can bring death or life;
   those who love to talk will reap the consequences.

²² The man who finds a wife finds a treasure,
   and he receives favor from the LORD.

²³ The poor plead for mercy;
   the rich answer with insults.

²⁴ There are "friends" who destroy each other,
   but a real friend sticks closer than a brother.

19 ¹ Better to be poor and honest
      than to be dishonest and a fool.

² Enthusiasm without knowledge is no good;
   haste makes mistakes.

³ People ruin their lives by their own foolishness
   and then are angry at the LORD.

⁴ Wealth makes many "friends";
   poverty drives them all away.

⁵ A false witness will not go unpunished,
   nor will a liar escape.

⁶ Many seek favors from a ruler;
   everyone is the friend of a person who gives gifts!

⁷ The relatives of the poor despise them;
   how much more will their friends avoid them!
Though the poor plead with them,
   their friends are gone.

⁸ *To acquire wisdom is to love yourself;*

   people who cherish understanding will prosper.

⁹ A false witness will not go unpunished,
   and a liar will be destroyed.

¹⁰ It isn't right for a fool to live in luxury
   or for a slave to rule over princes!

¹¹ Sensible people control their temper;
   they earn respect by overlooking wrongs.

¹² The king's anger is like a lion's roar,
   but his favor is like dew on the grass.

¹³ A foolish child is a calamity to a father;
   a quarrelsome wife is as annoying as constant
      dripping.

14 Fathers can give their sons an inheritance of houses and wealth,
but only the Lord can give an understanding wife.

15 Lazy people sleep soundly,
but idleness leaves them hungry.

16 Keep the commandments and keep your life;
despising them leads to death.

17 If you help the poor, you are lending to the Lord—
and he will repay you!

18 Discipline your children while there is hope.
Otherwise you will ruin their lives.

19 Hot-tempered people must pay the penalty.
If you rescue them once, you will have to do it again.

20 Get all the *advice and instruction* you can,
so you will be *wise* the rest of your *life.*

21 *You* can make *many plans,*
but the *LORD'S purpose* will prevail.

22 Loyalty makes a person attractive.
It is better to be poor than dishonest.

23 Fear of the Lord leads to life,
bringing security and protection from harm.

24 Lazy people take food in their hand
but don't even lift it to their mouth.

25 If you punish a mocker, the simpleminded will learn a lesson;
if you correct the wise, they will be all the wiser.

26 Children who mistreat their father or chase away their mother
are an embarrassment and a public disgrace.

27 If you stop listening to instruction, my child,
you will turn your back on knowledge.

28 A corrupt witness makes a mockery of justice;
the mouth of the wicked gulps down evil.

29 Punishment is made for mockers,
and the backs of fools are made to be beaten.

You CAN MAKE many plans, BUT THE LORD'S purpose WILL PREVAIL.
PROVERBS 19:21

20 ¹ Wine produces mockers; alcohol leads to brawls.
Those led astray by drink cannot be wise.

² The king's fury is like a lion's roar;
to rouse his anger is to risk your life.

³ Avoiding a fight is a mark of honor;
only fools insist on quarreling.

⁴ Those too lazy to plow in the right season
will have no food at the harvest.

⁵ Though good advice lies deep within the heart,
a person with understanding will draw it out.

⁶ Many will say they are loyal friends,
but who can find one who is truly reliable?

⁷ The godly walk with integrity;
blessed are their children who follow them.

⁸ When a king sits in judgment, he weighs all the evidence,
distinguishing the bad from the good.

⁹ Who can say, "I have cleansed my heart;
I am pure and free from sin"?

¹⁰ False weights and unequal measures—
the LORD detests double standards of every kind.

¹¹ Even children are known by the way they act,
whether their conduct is pure, and whether it is right.

¹² Ears to hear and eyes to see—
both are gifts from the LORD.

¹³ If you love sleep, you will end in poverty.
Keep your eyes open, and there will be plenty to eat!

¹⁴ The buyer haggles over the price, saying, "It's worthless,"
then brags about getting a bargain!

¹⁵ *Wise words* are more *valuable*
than much *gold* and many *rubies.*

¹⁶ Get security from someone who guarantees a stranger's debt.
Get a deposit if he does it for foreigners.

¹⁷ Stolen bread tastes sweet,
but it turns to gravel in the mouth.

¹⁸ Plans succeed through good counsel;
don't go to war without wise advice.

¹⁹ A gossip goes around telling secrets,
so don't hang around with chatterers.

²⁰ If you insult your father or mother,
your light will be snuffed out in total darkness.

²¹ An inheritance obtained too early in life
is not a blessing in the end.

The **godly** **walk** WITH *integrity;* **BLESSED** ARE THEIR CHILDREN WHO FOLLOW THEM.

PROVERBS 20:7

²² Don't say, "I will get even for this wrong."
    Wait for the LORD to handle the matter.

²³ The LORD detests double standards;
    he is not pleased by dishonest scales.

²⁴ *The LORD directs our steps,*

so why try to understand everything along the way?

²⁵ Don't trap yourself by making a rash promise to God
    and only later counting the cost.

²⁶ A wise king scatters the wicked like wheat,
    then runs his threshing wheel over them.

²⁷ The LORD's light penetrates the human spirit,
    exposing every hidden motive.

²⁸ Unfailing love and faithfulness protect the king;
    his throne is made secure through love.

²⁹ The glory of the young is their strength;
    the gray hair of experience is the splendor of the old.

³⁰ Physical punishment cleanses away evil;
    such discipline purifies the heart.

21 ¹ The king's heart is like a stream of water directed by the LORD;
        he guides it wherever he pleases.

² People may be right in their own eyes,
    but the LORD examines their heart.

³ *The LORD is more pleased when we do what is*

right and just than when we offer him sacrifices.

⁴ Haughty eyes, a proud heart,
    and evil actions are all sin.

⁵ Good planning and hard work lead to prosperity,
    but hasty shortcuts lead to poverty.

⁶ Wealth created by a lying tongue
    is a vanishing mist and a deadly trap.

⁷ The violence of the wicked sweeps them away,
    because they refuse to do what is just.

⁸ The guilty walk a crooked path;
    the innocent travel a straight road.

⁹ It's better to live alone in the corner of an attic
    than with a quarrelsome wife in a lovely home.

¹⁰ Evil people desire evil;
    their neighbors get no mercy from them.

¹¹ If you punish a mocker, the simpleminded become wise;
   if you instruct the wise, they will be all the wiser.

¹² The Righteous One knows what is going on in the homes of the wicked;
   he will bring disaster on them.

¹³ Those who shut their ears to the cries of the poor
   will be ignored in their own time of need.

¹⁴ A secret gift calms anger;
   a bribe under the table pacifies fury.

¹⁵ Justice is a joy to the godly,
   but it terrifies evildoers.

¹⁶ The person who strays from common sense
   will end up in the company of the dead.

¹⁷ Those who love pleasure become poor;
   those who love wine and luxury will never be rich.

¹⁸ The wicked are punished in place of the godly,
   and traitors in place of the honest.

¹⁹ It's better to live alone in the desert
   than with a quarrelsome, complaining wife.

²⁰ The wise have wealth and luxury,
   but fools spend whatever they get.

²¹ Whoever pursues *righteousness* and unfailing *love*

   will find *life, righteousness,* and *honor.*

²² The wise conquer the city of the strong
   and level the fortress in which they trust.

²³ Watch your tongue and keep your mouth shut,
   and you will stay out of trouble.

²⁴ Mockers are proud and haughty;
   they act with boundless arrogance.

²⁵ Despite their desires, the lazy will come to ruin,
   for their hands refuse to work.

²⁶ Some people are always greedy for more,
   but the godly love to give!

²⁷ The sacrifice of an evil person is detestable,
   especially when it is offered with wrong motives.

²⁸ A false witness will be cut off,
   but a credible witness will be allowed to speak.

²⁹ The wicked bluff their way through,
   but the virtuous think before they act.

³⁰ No human wisdom or understanding or plan
   can stand against the LORD.

³¹ The horse is prepared for the day of battle,
   but the victory belongs to the LORD.

WHOEVER PURSUES RIGHTEOUSNESS AND unfailing LOVE WILL FIND life, RIGHTEOUSNESS, and HONOR.

PROVERBS 21:21

22 [1] Choose a good reputation over great riches;
    being held in high esteem is better than silver or gold.

[2] The rich and poor have this in common:
    The Lord made them both.

[3] A prudent person foresees danger and takes precautions.
    The simpleton goes blindly on and suffers the consequences.

[4] *True humility* and fear of *the Lord*

    lead to *riches, honor, and long life.*

[5] Corrupt people walk a thorny, treacherous road;
    whoever values life will avoid it.

[6] Direct your children onto the right path,
    and when they are older, they will not leave it.

[7] Just as the rich rule the poor,
    so the borrower is servant to the lender.

[8] Those who plant injustice will harvest disaster,
    and their reign of terror will come to an end.

[9] *Blessed* are those who are *generous,*

    because they feed the poor.

[10] Throw out the mocker, and fighting goes, too.
    Quarrels and insults will disappear.

[11] Whoever loves a pure heart and gracious speech
    will have the king as a friend.

[12] The Lord preserves those with knowledge,
    but he ruins the plans of the treacherous.

[13] The lazy person claims, "There's a lion out there!
    If I go outside, I might be killed!"

[14] The mouth of an immoral woman is a dangerous trap;
    those who make the Lord angry will fall into it.

[15] A youngster's heart is filled with foolishness,
    but physical discipline will drive it far away.

[16] A person who gets ahead by oppressing the poor
    or by showering gifts on the rich will end in poverty.

Sayings of the Wise

[17] Listen to the words of the wise;
    apply your heart to my instruction.

[18] For it is *good to keep* these sayings in *your heart*

    and always ready on *your lips.*

[19] I am teaching you today—yes, you—
    so you will trust in the Lord.

20 I have written thirty sayings for you,
   filled with advice and knowledge.
21 In this way, you may know the truth
   and take an accurate report to those who sent you.

22 Don't rob the poor just because you can,
   or exploit the needy in court.
23 For the LORD is their defender.
   He will ruin anyone who ruins them.

24 Don't befriend angry people
   or associate with hot-tempered people,
25 or you will learn to be like them
   and endanger your soul.

26 Don't agree to guarantee another person's debt
   or put up security for someone else.
27 If you can't pay it,
   even your bed will be snatched from under you.

28 Don't cheat your neighbor by moving the ancient boundary markers
   set up by previous generations.

29 Do you see any truly competent workers?
   They will serve kings
   rather than working for ordinary people.

23 **1** While dining with a ruler,
   pay attention to what is put before you.
2 If you are a big eater,
   put a knife to your throat;
3 don't desire all the delicacies,
   for he might be trying to trick you.

4 Don't wear yourself out trying to get rich.
   Be wise enough to know when to quit.
5 In the blink of an eye wealth disappears,
   for it will sprout wings
   and fly away like an eagle.

6 Don't eat with people who are stingy;
   don't desire their delicacies.
7 They are always thinking about how much it costs.
   "Eat and drink," they say, but they don't mean it.
8 You will throw up what little you've eaten,
   and your compliments will be wasted.

9 Don't waste your breath on fools,
   for they will despise the wisest advice.

10 Don't cheat your neighbor by moving the ancient boundary markers;
   don't take the land of defenseless orphans.
11 For their Redeemer is strong;
   he himself will bring their charges against you.

12 *Commit yourself to instruction;*
   listen carefully to words of knowledge.

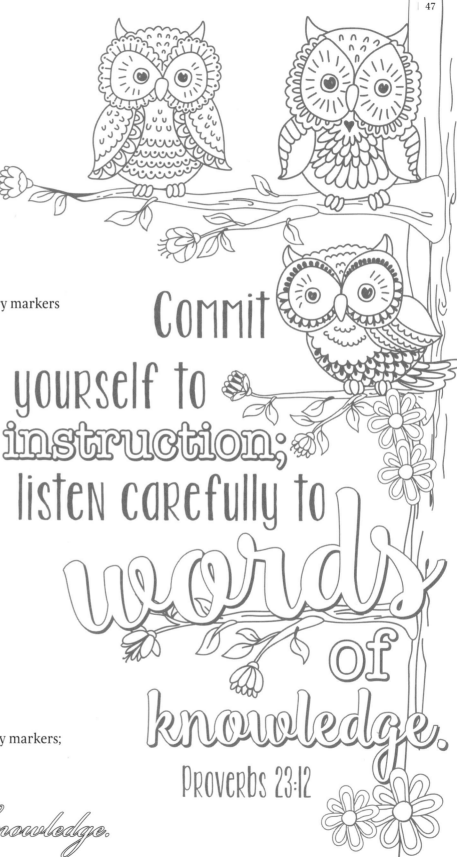

Commit yourself to instruction; listen carefully to words of knowledge.

Proverbs 23:12

[13] Don't fail to discipline your children.
  The rod of punishment won't kill them.
[14] Physical discipline
  may well save them from death.

[15] My child, if your heart is wise,
  my own heart will rejoice!
[16] Everything in me will celebrate
  when you speak what is right.

[17] Don't envy sinners,
  but always continue to fear the Lord.
[18] You will be rewarded for this;
  your hope will not be disappointed.

[19] *My child*, listen and *be wise:*

Keep your *heart* on the right course.

[20] Do not carouse with drunkards
  or feast with gluttons,
[21] for they are on their way to poverty,
  and too much sleep clothes them in rags.

[22] Listen to your father, who gave you life,
  and don't despise your mother when she is old.
[23] Get the truth and never sell it;
  also get wisdom, discipline, and good judgment.
[24] The father of godly children has cause for joy.
  What a pleasure to have children who are wise.
[25] So give your father and mother joy!
  May she who gave you birth be happy.

[26] O my son, give me your heart.
  May your eyes take delight in following my ways.
[27] A prostitute is a dangerous trap;
  a promiscuous woman is as dangerous as falling into
    a narrow well.
[28] She hides and waits like a robber,
  eager to make more men unfaithful.

[29] Who has anguish? Who has sorrow?
  Who is always fighting? Who is always complaining?
  Who has unnecessary bruises? Who has bloodshot eyes?
[30] It is the one who spends long hours in the taverns,
  trying out new drinks.
[31] Don't gaze at the wine, seeing how red it is,
  how it sparkles in the cup, how smoothly it goes down.
[32] For in the end it bites like a poisonous snake;
  it stings like a viper.
[33] You will see hallucinations,
  and you will say crazy things.
[34] You will stagger like a sailor tossed at sea,
  clinging to a swaying mast.

The father of *godly children* has cause for JOY. What a pleasure to have CHILDREN who are *wise.*

Proverbs 23:24

[35] And you will say, "They hit me, but I didn't feel it.
  I didn't even know it when they beat me up.
  When will I wake up
    so I can look for another drink?"

24 [1] Don't envy evil people
    or desire their company.
[2] For their hearts plot violence,
  and their words always stir up trouble.

[3] A house is built by wisdom
  and becomes strong through good sense.
[4] Through knowledge its rooms are filled
  with all sorts of precious riches and valuables.

[5] *The wise are mightier than the strong,*

and those with knowledge grow stronger and stronger.

[6] So don't go to war without wise guidance;
  victory depends on having many advisers.

[7] Wisdom is too lofty for fools.
  Among leaders at the city gate, they have nothing
    to say.

A HOUSE IS BUILT BY wisdom & BECOMES STRONG THROUGH GOOD SENSE.

⁸ A person who plans evil
    will get a reputation as a troublemaker.
⁹ The schemes of a fool are sinful;
    everyone detests a mocker.

¹⁰ If you fail under pressure,
    your strength is too small.

¹¹ Rescue those who are unjustly sentenced to die;
    save them as they stagger to their death.
¹² Don't excuse yourself by saying, "Look, we didn't know."
    For God understands all hearts, and he sees you.
    He who guards your soul knows you knew.
    He will repay all people as their actions deserve.

¹³ My child, eat honey, for it is good,
    and the honeycomb is sweet to the taste.

¹⁴ *In the same way, wisdom is sweet to your soul.*

If you find it, you will have a bright future,

and your hopes will not be cut short.

¹⁵ Don't wait in ambush at the home of the godly,
    and don't raid the house where the godly live.
¹⁶ The godly may trip seven times, but they will get up again.
    But one disaster is enough to overthrow the wicked.

THROUGH knowledge ITS ROOMS ARE FILLED WITH ALL SORTS OF precious riches & VALUABLES.

PROVERBS 24:3-4

¹⁷ Don't rejoice when your enemies fall;
   don't be happy when they stumble.
¹⁸ For the Lord will be displeased with you
   and will turn his anger away from them.

¹⁹ Don't fret because of evildoers;
   don't envy the wicked.
²⁰ For evil people have no future;
   the light of the wicked will be snuffed out.

²¹ My child, fear the Lord and the king.
   Don't associate with rebels,
²² for disaster will hit them suddenly.
   Who knows what punishment will come
   from the Lord and the king?

More Sayings of the Wise
²³Here are some further sayings of the wise:

  It is wrong to show favoritism when passing judgment.
²⁴ A judge who says to the wicked, "You are innocent,"
   will be cursed by many people and denounced by the
     nations.
²⁵ But it will go well for those who convict the guilty;
   rich blessings will be showered on them.

²⁶ *An honest answer is like a kiss of friendship.*

²⁷ Do your planning and prepare your fields
   before building your house.

²⁸ Don't testify against your neighbors without cause;
   don't lie about them.
²⁹ And don't say, "Now I can pay them back for what they've done to me!
   I'll get even with them!"

³⁰ I walked by the field of a lazy person,
   the vineyard of one with no common sense.
³¹ I saw that it was overgrown with nettles.
   It was covered with weeds,
   and its walls were broken down.
³² Then, as I looked and thought about it,
   I learned this lesson:
³³ A little extra sleep, a little more slumber,
   a little folding of the hands to rest—
³⁴ then poverty will pounce on you like a bandit;
   scarcity will attack you like an armed robber.

TIMELY advice is lovely, like golden apples in a silver basket.

Proverbs 25:11

More Proverbs of Solomon

25 These are more proverbs of Solomon, collected by the advisers of King Hezekiah of Judah.

² It is God's privilege to conceal things
    and the king's privilege to discover them.

³ No one can comprehend the height of heaven, the depth of the earth,
    or all that goes on in the king's mind!

⁴ Remove the impurities from silver,
    and the sterling will be ready for the silversmith.
⁵ Remove the wicked from the king's court,
    and his reign will be made secure by justice.

⁶ Don't demand an audience with the king
    or push for a place among the great.
⁷ It's better to wait for an invitation to the head table
    than to be sent away in public disgrace.

  Just because you've seen something,
⁸   don't be in a hurry to go to court.
  For what will you do in the end
    if your neighbor deals you a shameful defeat?

⁹ When arguing with your neighbor,
    don't betray another person's secret.
¹⁰ Others may accuse you of gossip,
    and you will never regain your good reputation.

¹¹ Timely advice is lovely,
    like golden apples in a silver basket.

¹² To one who listens, valid criticism
    is like a gold earring or other gold jewelry.

¹³  *Trustworthy messengers refresh like snow in summer.*
    They revive the spirit of their employer.

¹⁴ A person who promises a gift but doesn't give it
    is like clouds and wind that bring no rain.

¹⁵ Patience can persuade a prince,
    and soft speech can break bones.

¹⁶ Do you like honey?
    Don't eat too much, or it will make you sick!

¹⁷ Don't visit your neighbors too often,
    or you will wear out your welcome.

¹⁸ Telling lies about others
    is as harmful as hitting them with an ax,
  wounding them with a sword,
    or shooting them with a sharp arrow.

¹⁹ Putting confidence in an unreliable person in times of trouble
    is like chewing with a broken tooth or walking on a lame foot.

20 Singing cheerful songs to a person with a heavy heart
　　is like taking someone's coat in cold weather
　　or pouring vinegar in a wound.

21 If your enemies are hungry, give them food to eat.
　　If they are thirsty, give them water to drink.
22 You will heap burning coals of shame on their heads,
　　and the Lord will reward you.

23 As surely as a north wind brings rain,
　　so a gossiping tongue causes anger!

24 It's better to live alone in the corner of an attic
　　than with a quarrelsome wife in a lovely home.

25 *Good news* from far away
　　　　is like cold water to *the thirsty*.

26 If the godly give in to the wicked,
　　it's like polluting a fountain or muddying a spring.

27 It's not good to eat too much honey,
　　and it's not good to seek honors for yourself.

28 A person without self-control
　　is like a city with broken-down walls.

26 **1** Honor is no more associated with fools
　　than snow with summer or rain with harvest.

2 Like a fluttering sparrow or a darting swallow,
　　an undeserved curse will not land on its intended victim.

3 Guide a horse with a whip, a donkey with a bridle,
　　and a fool with a rod to his back!

4 Don't answer the foolish arguments of fools,
　　or you will become as foolish as they are.

5 Be sure to answer the foolish arguments of fools,
　　or they will become wise in their own estimation.

6 Trusting a fool to convey a message
　　is like cutting off one's feet or drinking poison!

7 A proverb in the mouth of a fool
　　is as useless as a paralyzed leg.

8 Honoring a fool
　　is as foolish as tying a stone to a slingshot.

9 A proverb in the mouth of a fool
　　is like a thorny branch brandished by a drunk.

10 An employer who hires a fool or a bystander
　　is like an archer who shoots at random.

11 As a dog returns to its vomit,
　　so a fool repeats his foolishness.

Good NEWS FROM FAR AWAY IS LIKE COLD WATER TO THE *Thirsty*

PROVERBS 25:25

[12] There is more hope for fools
    than for people who think they are wise.

[13] The lazy person claims, "There's a lion on the road!
    Yes, I'm sure there's a lion out there!"

[14] As a door swings back and forth on its hinges,
    so the lazy person turns over in bed.

[15] Lazy people take food in their hand
    but don't even lift it to their mouth.

[16] Lazy people consider themselves smarter
    than seven wise counselors.

[17] Interfering in someone else's argument
    is as foolish as yanking a dog's ears.

[18] Just as damaging
    as a madman shooting a deadly weapon
[19] is someone who lies to a friend
    and then says, "I was only joking."

[20] Fire goes out without wood,
    and quarrels disappear when gossip stops.

[21] A quarrelsome person starts fights
    as easily as hot embers light charcoal or fire lights wood.

[22] Rumors are dainty morsels
    that sink deep into one's heart.

[23] Smooth words may hide a wicked heart,
    just as a pretty glaze covers a clay pot.

[24] People may cover their hatred with pleasant words,
    but they're deceiving you.
[25] They pretend to be kind, but don't believe them.
    Their hearts are full of many evils.
[26] While their hatred may be concealed by trickery,
    their wrongdoing will be exposed in public.

[27] If you set a trap for others,
    you will get caught in it yourself.
If you roll a boulder down on others,
    it will crush you instead.

[28] A lying tongue hates its victims,
    and flattering words cause ruin.

27 [1] Don't brag about tomorrow,
    since you don't know what the day will bring.

[2] Let someone else praise you, not your own mouth—
    a stranger, not your own lips.

[3] A stone is heavy and sand is weighty,
    but the resentment caused by a fool is even heavier.

[4] Anger is cruel, and wrath is like a flood,
    but jealousy is even more dangerous.

⁵ An open rebuke
   is better than hidden love!

⁶ Wounds from a sincere friend
   are better than many kisses from an enemy.

⁷ A person who is full refuses honey,
   but even bitter food tastes sweet to the hungry.

⁸ A person who strays from home
   is like a bird that strays from its nest.

⁹ *The heartfelt* counsel of a *friend*

   is as *sweet as perfume* and incense.

¹⁰ Never abandon a friend—
   either yours or your father's.
   When disaster strikes, you won't have to ask your brother for assistance.
   It's better to go to a neighbor than to a brother who lives far away.

¹¹ Be wise, my child, and make my heart glad.
   Then I will be able to answer my critics.

¹² A prudent person foresees danger and takes precautions.
   The simpleton goes blindly on and suffers the consequences.

¹³ Get security from someone who guarantees a stranger's debt.
   Get a deposit if he does it for foreigners.

¹⁴ A loud and cheerful greeting early in the morning
   will be taken as a curse!

¹⁵ A quarrelsome wife is as annoying
   as constant dripping on a rainy day.
¹⁶ Stopping her complaints is like trying to stop the wind
   or trying to hold something with greased hands.

¹⁷ As *iron sharpens iron,*

   so a *friend sharpens a friend.*

¹⁸ As workers who tend a fig tree are allowed to eat the fruit,
   so workers who protect their employer's interests will be rewarded.

¹⁹ *As a face* is reflected in water,

   so the *heart* reflects the *real person.*

²⁰ Just as Death and Destruction are never satisfied,
   so human desire is never satisfied.

²¹ Fire tests the purity of silver and gold,
   but a person is tested by being praised.

The heartfelt counsel of a FRIEND is as sweet as perfume and INCENSE.

Proverbs 27:9

²² You cannot separate fools from their foolishness,
 even though you grind them like grain with mortar and
  pestle.

²³ Know the state of your flocks,
 and put your heart into caring for your herds,
²⁴ for riches don't last forever,
 and the crown might not be passed to the next generation.
²⁵ After the hay is harvested and the new crop appears
 and the mountain grasses are gathered in,
²⁶ your sheep will provide wool for clothing,
 and your goats will provide the price of a field.
²⁷ And you will have enough goats' milk for yourself,
 your family, and your servant girls.

28 ¹ The wicked run away when no one is chasing them,
 but the godly are as bold as lions.

² When there is moral rot within a nation, its government topples easily.
 But wise and knowledgeable leaders bring stability.

³ A poor person who oppresses the poor
 is like a pounding rain that destroys the crops.

⁴ To reject the law is to praise the wicked;
 to obey the law is to fight them.

⁵ Evil people don't understand justice,
 but those who follow the LORD understand completely.

⁶ *Better* to be poor and *honest*
 than to be dishonest and *rich.*

⁷ Young people who obey the law are wise;
 those with wild friends bring shame to their parents.

⁸ Income from charging high interest rates
 will end up in the pocket of someone who is kind to the poor.

⁹ God detests the prayers
 of a person who ignores the law.

¹⁰ Those who lead good people along an evil path
 will fall into their own trap,
 but the honest will inherit good things.

¹¹ Rich people may think they are wise,
 but a poor person with discernment can see right through them.

¹² When the godly succeed, everyone is glad.
 When the wicked take charge, people go into hiding.

¹³ People who conceal their sins will not prosper,
 but if they confess and turn from them, they will receive mercy.

¹⁴ *Blessed* are those who *fear to do wrong,*

 but the stubborn are headed for serious trouble.

Discipline *your* children, & they will *give* you PEACE of mind and will make your *heart* GLAD.

Proverbs 29:17

15 A wicked ruler is as dangerous to the poor
  as a roaring lion or an attacking bear.

16 A ruler with no understanding will oppress his people,
  but one who hates corruption will have a long life.

17 A murderer's tormented conscience will drive him into the grave.
  Don't protect him!

18 The blameless will be rescued from harm,
  but the crooked will be suddenly destroyed.

19 A hard worker has plenty of food,
  but a person who chases fantasies ends up in poverty.

20 The trustworthy person will get a rich reward,
  but a person who wants quick riches will get into
    trouble.

21 Showing partiality is never good,
  yet some will do wrong for a mere piece of bread.

22 Greedy people try to get rich quick
  but don't realize they're headed for poverty.

23 In the end, people appreciate honest criticism
  far more than flattery.

24 Anyone who steals from his father and mother
  and says, "What's wrong with that?"
  is no better than a murderer.

25 *Greed causes fighting;*

trusting the LORD leads to prosperity.

26 Those who trust their own insight are foolish,
  but anyone who walks in wisdom is safe.

27 Whoever gives to the poor will lack nothing,
  but those who close their eyes to poverty will be cursed.

28 When the wicked take charge, people go into hiding.
  When the wicked meet disaster, the godly flourish.

Whoever *gives* to the poor will lack nothing.
Proverbs 28:27

29

¹ Whoever stubbornly refuses to accept criticism
will suddenly be destroyed beyond recovery.

² When the godly are in authority, the people rejoice.
But when the wicked are in power, they groan.

³ The man who loves wisdom brings joy to his father,
but if he hangs around with prostitutes, his wealth is
wasted.

⁴ A just king gives stability to his nation,
but one who demands bribes destroys it.

⁵ To flatter friends
is to lay a trap for their feet.

⁶ Evil people are trapped by sin,
but the righteous escape, shouting for joy.

⁷ The godly care about the rights of the poor;
the wicked don't care at all.

⁸ Mockers can get a whole town agitated,
but the wise will calm anger.

⁹ If a wise person takes a fool to court,
there will be ranting and ridicule but no
satisfaction.

¹⁰ The bloodthirsty hate blameless people,
but the upright seek to help them.

¹¹ Fools vent their anger,
but the wise quietly hold it back.

¹² If a ruler pays attention to liars,
all his advisers will be wicked.

¹³ The poor and the oppressor have this in common—
the LORD gives sight to the eyes of both.

¹⁴ If a king judges the poor fairly,
his throne will last forever.

¹⁵ To discipline a child produces wisdom,
but a mother is disgraced by an undisciplined child.

¹⁶ When the wicked are in authority, sin flourishes,
but the godly will live to see their downfall.

¹⁷ Discipline your children, and they will give you peace of mind
and will make your heart glad.

¹⁸ When people do not accept divine guidance, they run wild.
But whoever obeys the law is joyful.

¹⁹ Words alone will not discipline a servant;
the words may be understood, but they are not heeded.

²⁰ There is more hope for a fool
than for someone who speaks without thinking.

²¹ A servant pampered from childhood
will become a rebel.

Who but **God** goes up to **HEAVEN** and comes back down? Who holds the wind in his fists? Who wraps up the oceans in his cloak? Who has *created* the whole wide *world?*

Proverbs 30:4

²² An angry person starts fights;
  a hot-tempered person commits all kinds of sin.

²³ *Pride* ends in humiliation,

  while humility brings *honor.*

²⁴ If you assist a thief, you only hurt yourself.
  You are sworn to tell the truth, but you dare not testify.

²⁵ Fearing people is a dangerous trap,
  but trusting the LORD means safety.

²⁶ Many seek the ruler's favor,
  but justice comes from the LORD.

²⁷ The righteous despise the unjust;
  the wicked despise the godly.

The Sayings of Agur

30 The sayings of Agur son of Jakeh contain this message.

  I am weary, O God;
    I am weary and worn out, O God.
² I am too stupid to be human,
    and I lack common sense.
³ I have not mastered human wisdom,
    nor do I know the Holy One.

⁴ Who but God goes up to heaven and comes back down?
    Who holds the wind in his fists?
  Who wraps up the oceans in his cloak?
    Who has created the whole wide world?
  What is his name—and his son's name?
    Tell me if you know!

⁵ *Every word of God* proves true.

  He is a shield to all who come to him for *protection.*

⁶ Do not add to his words,
    or he may rebuke you and expose you as a liar.

⁷ O God, I beg two favors from you;
    let me have them before I die.
⁸ First, help me never to tell a lie.
    Second, give me neither poverty nor riches!
    Give me just enough to satisfy my needs.
⁹ For if I grow rich, I may deny you and say, "Who is the LORD?"
    And if I am too poor, I may steal and thus insult God's holy name.

¹⁰ Never slander a worker to the employer,
    or the person will curse you, and you will pay for it.

¹¹ Some people curse their father
   and do not thank their mother.
¹² They are pure in their own eyes,
   but they are filthy and unwashed.
¹³ They look proudly around,
   casting disdainful glances.
¹⁴ They have teeth like swords
   and fangs like knives.
 They devour the poor from the earth
   and the needy from among humanity.

¹⁵ The leech has two suckers
   that cry out, "More, more!"

 There are three things that are never satisfied—
   no, four that never say, "Enough!":
¹⁶ the grave,
   the barren womb,
   the thirsty desert,
   the blazing fire.

¹⁷ The eye that mocks a father
   and despises a mother's instructions
 will be plucked out by ravens of the valley
   and eaten by vultures.

¹⁸ *There are* three things that *amaze me*—
   no, four things that I don't understand:
¹⁹ how an eagle glides through the sky,
   how a snake slithers on a rock,
   how a ship navigates the ocean,
   how a man loves a woman.

²⁰ An adulterous woman consumes a man,
   then wipes her mouth and says, "What's wrong with that?"

²¹ *There are* three things that
 make the *earth tremble*—
   no, four it cannot endure:
²² a slave who becomes a king,
   an overbearing fool who prospers,
²³   a bitter woman who finally gets a husband,
   a servant girl who supplants her mistress.

²⁴ *There are* four things on earth that
   are small but unusually *wise:*

²⁵ Ants—they aren't strong,
   but they store up food all summer.
²⁶ Hyraxes—they aren't powerful,
   but they make their homes among the rocks.

SHE IS CLOTHED WITH *strength* AND *dignity,* & SHE LAUGHS WITHOUT FEAR OF THE FUTURE. WHEN SHE SPEAKS, HER WORDS ARE WISE, AND SHE GIVES *instructions* WITH *kindness.*

PROVERBS 31:25-26

You ARE more precious THAN rubies

PROVERBS 31:10

27 Locusts—they have no king,
  but they march in formation.
28 Lizards—they are easy to catch,
  but they are found even in kings' palaces.

29 *There are* three things that
  walk with stately stride—
  no, four that strut about:
30 the lion, king of animals, who won't turn aside for anything,
31 the strutting rooster,
  the male goat,
  a king as he leads his army.

32 If you have been a fool by being proud or plotting evil,
  cover your mouth in shame.

33 As the beating of cream yields butter
  and striking the nose causes bleeding,
  so stirring up anger causes quarrels.

The Sayings of King Lemuel

31 The sayings of King Lemuel contain this message, which his mother taught him.

2 O my son, O son of my womb,
  O son of my vows,
3 do not waste your strength on women,
  on those who ruin kings.

4 It is not for kings, O Lemuel, to guzzle wine.
  Rulers should not crave alcohol.
5 For if they drink, they may forget the law
  and not give justice to the oppressed.
6 Alcohol is for the dying,
  and wine for those in bitter distress.
7 Let them drink to forget their poverty
  and remember their troubles no more.

8 Speak up for those who cannot speak for themselves;
  ensure justice for those being crushed.
9 Yes, speak up for the poor and helpless,
  and see that they get justice.

A Wife of Noble Character

10 *Who can find a virtuous and capable wife?*
  She is more precious than rubies.

11 Her husband can trust her,
  and she will greatly enrich his life.
12 She brings him good, not harm,
  all the days of her life.

¹³ She finds wool and flax
    and busily spins it.
¹⁴ She is like a merchant's ship,
    bringing her food from afar.
¹⁵ She gets up before dawn to prepare breakfast for her
      household
    and plan the day's work for her servant girls.

¹⁶ She goes to inspect a field and buys it;
    with her earnings she plants a vineyard.
¹⁷ She is energetic and strong,
    a hard worker.
¹⁸ She makes sure her dealings are profitable;
    her lamp burns late into the night.

¹⁹ Her hands are busy spinning thread,
    her fingers twisting fiber.
²⁰ She extends a helping hand to the poor
    and opens her arms to the needy.
²¹ She has no fear of winter for her household,
    for everyone has warm clothes.

²² She makes her own bedspreads.
    She dresses in fine linen and purple gowns.
²³ Her husband is well known at the city gates,
    where he sits with the other civic leaders.
²⁴ She makes belted linen garments
    and sashes to sell to the merchants.

²⁵ She is clothed with strength and dignity,
    and she laughs without fear of the future.
²⁶ When she speaks, her words are wise,
    and she gives instructions with kindness.
²⁷ She carefully watches everything in her household
    and suffers nothing from laziness.

²⁸ *Her children* stand and *bless her.*

Her husband praises her:

²⁹ "There are many virtuous and capable women in the world,
    but you surpass them all!"

³⁰ *Charm* is deceptive, and ***beauty*** does not last;

but a ***woman*** who fears *the LORD* will be *greatly praised.*

³¹ Reward her for all she has done.
    Let her deeds publicly declare her praise.

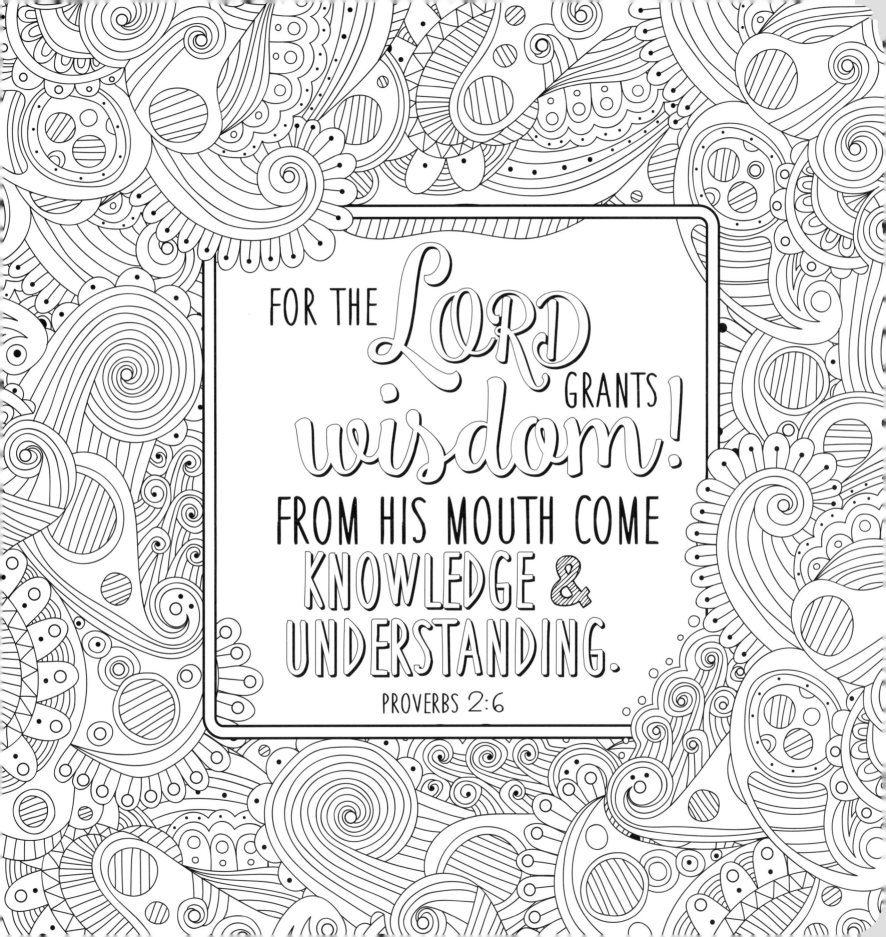

Never let loyalty & kindness leave you! Tie them around your neck as a reminder. Write them deep within your heart.

Proverbs 3:3

TRUST in the LORD with all your HEART; do not depend on your own understanding. Seek his will in all you do, & he will show you which PATH to take. Proverbs 3:5-6

The way of the righteous is like the first gleam of dawn, which shines ever brighter until the full light of day.

Proverbs 4:18

MARK OUT a STRAIGHT PATH for your feet; stay on the safe path.

Proverbs 4:26

For
WISDOM
is far more *valuable*
than rubies.
Nothing you desire
can compare with it.

Proverbs 8:11

Fear of the **Lord** is the foundation of WISDOM. Knowledge of the *Holy One* results in good judgment.

Proverbs 9:10

WISE

words bring many benefits,
and hard work brings rewards.

Proverbs 12:14

HER CHILDREN STAND & *bless* her. HER HUSBAND praises her: "THERE ARE MANY VIRTUOUS AND CAPABLE WOMEN IN THE WORLD, BUT YOU surpass *them all!*"

Proverbs 31:28-29

FOLD

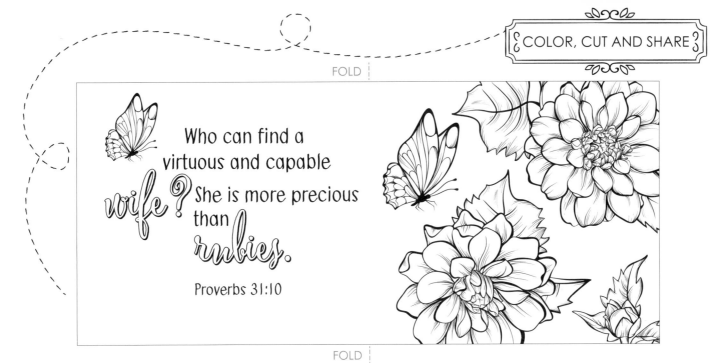

Who can find a virtuous and capable *wife*? She is more precious than *rubies.*

Proverbs 31:10

FOLD

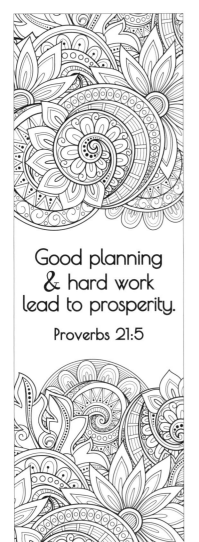

Good planning & hard work lead to prosperity.

Proverbs 21:5

Kind words are like *honey* — sweet to the soul and healthy for the body.

Proverbs 16:24

The name of the LORD is a strong fortress; the godly run to him and are *safe.*

Proverbs 18:10

FOLD

The
heartfelt
counsel of a friend is
as sweet as
perfume and incense.

Proverbs 27:9

FOLD

Those who
fear
the LORD are
secure; he will be a
refuge
for their children.

Proverbs 14:26

You can make
many
plans,
but the
LORD's
purpose
will prevail.

Proverbs 19:21

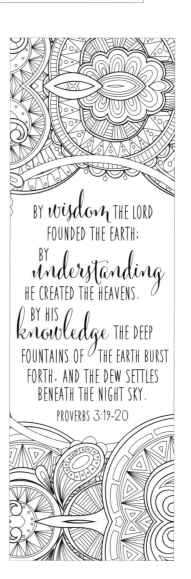

BY *wisdom* THE LORD
FOUNDED THE EARTH;
BY
understanding
HE CREATED THE HEAVENS.
BY HIS
knowledge THE DEEP
FOUNTAINS OF THE EARTH BURST
FORTH, AND THE DEW SETTLES
BENEATH THE NIGHT SKY.

PROVERBS 3:19-20

FOLD

A woman
who fears the LORD
will be greatly
praised.
Proverbs 31:30

Proverbs 31:10

*You are
more precious
than rubies!*

Those who trust the LORD
will be joyful.
Proverbs 16:20

FOLD

FOLD

TRUST in the LORD with all your HEART.

Proverbs 3:5

Commit your actions to the LORD, and your plans will succeed.

Proverbs 16:3

FOLD